Impressions from Yonder Soul

Truth & Belief

Choice & Intuition

Impressions from Yonder Soul

Truth & Belief

Choice & Intuition

David DiPietro Weiss

Impressions from Yonder Soul—
Truth & Belief, Choice & Intuition

Copyright © 2015 by David DiPietro Weiss

All rights reserved. No part of this book may be reproduced, stored in a retrieval system, or transmitted, in any form or by any means, electronic, mechanical, photocopying, recording, or otherwise, without the written prior permission of the author, except in the case of brief quotations embodied in critical articles and reviews.

ISBN 978-1-935914-44-0
Cover and Interior Design by River Sanctuary Graphic Arts

Printed in the United States of America

To order additional copies please visit:
www.riversanctuarypublishing.com

River Sanctuary Publishing
P.O Box 1561
Felton, CA 95018
www.riversanctuarypublishing.com
Dedicated to the Awakening of the New Earth

Contents

Preface i

Impressions from Yonder Soul 1

    Awareness—A First Step 11

    Intuition, Trust & Inspiration 13

    The Purposeful Inquiry 15

    Practice & Manifestation 19

    Truth and Belief 21

Truth #1—We are Eternal Spiritual Beings Temporarily Expressing Through a Physical Body 27

Truth #2—This is Not our First Appearance in a Physical Form 29

Truth #3—There's Only *ONE* of Us Here! 33

Truth #4—There are only Two Emotions on our Third Dimensional Plane, Love and Fear 35

Truth #5 — There is Only *NOW* 39

Truth #6 — Life Proceeds According to Our
Intention For It! 43

Truth #7 — You Must be Selfish Enough to Align
with Well-being 47

Truth #8 — The Law of Attraction is the Most Powerful
Law in the Universe 49

Truth #9 — Happiness Arises through Meditation
and Prayer 51

A Suggested Meditative Journey of Light 53

Truth #10 — You Are on the Correct Path 55

Epilogue: Our Soul Virtues 57

My Virtues of Spirit 59

Integral Thoughts to Enlightenment — 72 Things I've
Learned…And Counting 61

A Pre-Meditation Prayer…*I Am That I Am* 71

Preface

The following work was inspired by our Oneness group that meets each Wednesday evening to discuss and contemplate the lessons from the book of the same name, by author Rasha. As of this writing we are in our 8th month of meeting on the incredible lessons that emanate from this channeled masterpiece. Our group numbers range from 13 to 18 on any given evening that begins with a welcoming prayer and a meditation.

The inspiration that this group provides to each of us is difficult to measure. What we do know is that such talking circles lead to a wide-ranging crescendo of thought and intuition from each member. All of us are spiritually richer for the experience.

After one meeting where we contemplated the subjects of truth and belief, followed by another that discussed the impact of choice and intuition, I found myself outside my body as I retired that evening. I woke in the wee hours of darkness, bombarded by inspiration, instruction, and advice that permeated my entire being. It was not one's usual thoughtful or active dream, but a definite feeling of a spiritual download wherein I was directed to write my thoughts.

After tossing and turning the entire night, I woke up with the direction to write what I had heard. So I sat down and let the words come. And come they did. When I seemed to have concluded the download, I sat and perused what I had written. It seemed as if some other hand, some other entity had guided my thoughts and driven my fingers. Most of the thoughts made absolute sense to me after I read what I had written. And as I reread the piece, I was immediately and intuitively referred to a group of writers, sages and sayings that had been part of my life for some time. I included their thoughts in this essay and credited the authors. The result of this episodic download is contained here in these pages.

After a series of thoughtful meanderings, I have suggested a daily reminder that I call *Virtues of Spirit*. These core virtues, such as gratitude, forgiveness, compassion, patience, and surrender, all rise and blend into an etheric perfume we can recognize as Universal Love. It is my hope that you might consider copying them from the text to carry with you as a daily reference and reminder to practice such virtues. They are included as an epilogue.

In addition, I have included a compilation of thoughts and inspirations that I felt were integral to my alignment with Spirit. Over the past few months I had taken as a hobby to write down these thoughts as I came across them and have included them here as a reminder to myself of some of the major aspects of a new reality. It is an incomplete list and will continue to grow as I grow. I include them here as a dynamic reminder to myself of some major aspects of a new reality. I hope you will enjoy them.

Finally, I have included a pre-meditation prayer *by Master Choa Kok Sui, Grandmaster of Pranic Healing and Arhatic Yoga,* called, *I Am That I Am*. We begin our meditations with this prayer before bathing in the eternal silence and connection to our authentic self into and above the 5th dimension.

David DiPietro Weiss

Impressions from Yonder Soul
Truth & Belief — Choice & Intuition

MAN CONTINUALLY ASSERTS THAT HE is the sole possessor of free will. He believes that as he lives in the three-dimensional world, he has the unabated power to choose his thoughts, his actions, and his deeds in virtually every moment of his earthly existence in this, the third dimension. Man further asserts that this free will is his own unique divine power, that does not reside within any other species, and that he has the power of choice over each and every action he takes in each and every moment he lives. Every thought, feeling, action or non-action is governed by his perceived ability to choose—in what he determines to be—his *God given* free will. This is man's view of his divine birthright.

When man chooses to follow this course of reasoning, one can assume and affirm that he also believes that he has the power to defy God's wishes and that he can override the perceived power of God and choose his own divine course. If that is so, then God's divine power cannot be omnipotent. Man's God thus becomes a God of limitations, an imperfect God created by man's imperfect thoughts. If man's God is so limited, then what kind of God could it be and what unique power might it possess? Certainly he cannot be the God that man's religions have sanctioned. Because if man has absolute free will and free choice, then our created God loses his aura of omnipotence and can no longer be bestowed the title of an omnipresent, omnipotent, all-powerful spirit.

Conversely, if God is indeed all powerful and omniscient as some men also purport him to be, and man further chooses to live in the supposition that man has free will, he is specifically subject only to God's omnipotent will and cannot actually have free will or free choice. Does not it follow then, that man's life and choices are pre-destined or pre-formed before his incarnation into this third dimensional plane on the planet earth? If that is so then doesn't it also follow that man's life is simply a predetermined drama where the script has already been written and man has become simply the actor in an ongoing complicated and perpetual drama wherein his own egoist thoughts have duped him into thinking he has free will and choice?

Both scenarios leave much to be desired when one embarks on a quest of spirituality in a sincere attempt to follow a path that leads to ascension from this earth plane to a more spiritually enlightened existence. With an intuitive sense of knowing, many choose to follow what they believe to be a path of enlightenment. Many believe that they have free will and have the power to make free choices in the moral decisions they make on a day to day basis. And because they live in a relative world, they appear to make choices regularly. They seem to make obvious choices, for example, between good and evil as delineated through their personal perceptions, all relative to one's individual limited understanding of the universe.

In short, we all live in a dualistic world. But are we, as individuals or groups, making those choices? If not us, who is? Is it our concept of *God*? If *God* is making the choices, what role do we, if any, have as human beings?

In seeking truth that can satisfy our longing Soul, we have to realize and remember that we are living in our own created illusion we call life. We have to consider that: (a) we are not the body. (b) We are not the emotions. (c) We are not the thoughts and, (d) we are not the mind. The mind is simply an instrument of our Soul. The universal truth is that we *are* the Soul. The Soul is the living spirit creature that we are, our *authentic self,* not the physical body that we carry with us. This is our eternal and universal truth. The Soul *Is* and lives before, during, and after the passing of the body, the thoughts, the finite mind, and emotions. The Soul is who we truly are. In our physical third dimensional existence, we *think* our mind, thoughts, body and emotions are who we are. All of these elements constitute our sense of self, our ego. Once we embark on spiritual awareness, we realize and begin to become aware of who we really are. The human dilemma becomes readily apparent. We find that we are not the ego and there is no self as we know it.

The *Truth* is, however, that we do have choices. And we *do* have free will. However, it is not what we think or perceive it to be when we only use our limited third dimensional faculties. Choice and free will do not occur as our physical limitations choose to believe them to occur. It is indeed a *truth* that we choose our lives. We choose our parents, our geography, our relatives, friends, cohorts and spirit helpers. All such initial choices are made by the Authentic Self—the Soul. In the Spirit Circle, a family Council of Spirits between lives, you decide, with the help of your Council, on the need, content, and script of your next incarnation. The incarnation planned, if necessary for you, will be to again attempt to learn those lessons one has not yet mastered in previous incarnations. Therefore, one must reincarnate and return to experience those non-soulful choices to carry out the Soul's intent decided in the Spirit Council. The incarnation is necessary because of the lingering separation that exists between the Soul, your incarnated body, and the Source, or God. This separation and the perception of duality keep us from our Source and prevent us from becoming reunited with our true self—Oneness.

Those formulative prescribed decisions are made in the *space between*, in the Spiritual Council between lives, with our spiritual family that some refer to as our *Monad*, co-existing in another dimension and vibration. These infinite advisors are with us at every level of existence, including *now*, in your present incarnation. Together you plan what the parameters of your next incarnated eperience will be on the earth or, perhaps, other planetary location. Your Council is one of eternal, loving, spiritual, companions who realize that we are all one entity, that we are Oneness, that *we* are part of God—and one with God. And, while this spiritual gathering is not the *highest* expression of God to the extent of the evolution or awareness of one's Soul, it is here, in this divine place, where one truly has the unimpeded taste of free will and free choice. Here one chooses to incarnate into one's selected physical form as one is free in spirit to choose what one needs to do in one's next life. One's entire Akashic record [1] is available for review in this spiritual dimension. And, in this spiritual realm, one gives direction for one's next life and sets the parameters of choice and experiences that can be utilized on the third dimensional physical plane because of the lessons learned or not learned in previous lives. Because of this unrestricted knowledge inherent in the Council of what lessons each individual needs to satisfy his karmic records, one can, with ample advice and consultation with one's spiritual family and a re-review of one's Akashic record, prescribe the life, and the Spirit Council's parameters of potential choices for your next life. These parameters are necessary in order to balance one's karmic record that has been hewed and distilled from the hundreds, or perhaps thousands, of previous lives one has experienced.

Once reincarnated into a new life form—the scripted drama designed by your Spirit Council—one's life presents the needed experiences for the body to reconcile choices with the Soul and ultimately to Source.

So why does one not remember the mistakes or failures in a previous life that would seemingly allow one to live the life *intended* by the Soul? Wouldn't it be a great deal simpler if one could recall those incidents in past lives so one could assuredly not make the same *mistakes* again? Perhaps not! Why then, would such a seemingly *logical* recollection not really be appropriate for us? The answer is not complicated. It is true that the new incarnate does not recall or remember any of the plans germinated from the Spirit Council during any incarnation. He does, however, have an *innate knowingness* of a higher dimension that permeates his thoughts, yet he doesn't comprehend the source or the meaning of this knowingness. He tends to listen to what he deems as *real*—those thoughts of fear and survival which are perpetuated by the ego and rooted in the third dimension.

Not remembering is truly a cosmic gift. The Soul gifts this forgetfulness so the third dimensional body can be free to make choices without the burden of knowing how those choices would turn out and thereby negate the *validity of an actual choice*. Knowing choices ahead of one's birth would not allow one the necessary earthly experiences we incarnated to explore but would effectively narrow or eliminate completely the element of choice for the third dimension. One would tend to modify his choices if he knew already knew the outcome of his actions. To not recall our past lives when reincarnated into a physical form gives us an unfettered choice to connect with Spirit and our Source in the *Now* to make the Soul's decision as we invoke our intuition. In that space between, our Soul and monadic family are there to help us choose the panorama of life experiences one needs in order to move from duality back to Oneness, to God.

The incarnate then goes about experiencing the life drama that was scripted in the Spirit Council, continually being presented situations and experiences that the incarnate needs to live through as agreed to in the Council. He remains, throughout his incarnation, consciously unaware of the soul's intentions made in the Council. However, these intentions and agreements of incarnate action by the Spirit Council are constantly and continually presented to the incarnate in the *Now*. Thus the incarnate is actually presented continual choice options. The Soul's intentions are communicated to the incarnate through *intuition,* the communication vehicle that is constantly broadcasting in high vibrational frequency to the incarnate. This intuitive connection one can label the *Jiminy Cricket syndrome*, in honor of Walt Disney's cricket-conscience character to Pinocchio. The incarnate may not listen to or follow the advice of that intuitive communication, but could instead follow the seemingly comfortable choices of the third dimensional ego.

The incarnate, however, feels the dichotomy of choice constantly in his daily life as each situation or experience presents itself, yet he continues to waffle between spirit choices and ego choices. He is only vaguely aware of his Oneness, the unity with all life. He is bombarded with choice options between the ego and the intuition of his Soul. The intuition, of course, is the Soul's higher frequency direction, reflecting the agreement brokered between lives in the Spirit Council.

We are thus continually given the opportunity to modify or eliminate the behavior that keeps us reincarnating over and over, oftentimes repeating the same set of repetitive circumstances and lessons, although perhaps in many different forms and guises, until we, in the physical realm, *choose* the spiritual intent determined together in our Spirit Council. Man, indeed, exercises choice. The constant opportunities to choose occur in each moment, yet man is ill-equipped to understand the significance of choosing his intuitive voice over that of his seductive ego. The significance is revealed only after he awakens and becomes aware of the existence of higher dimensions and vibrations and realizes the falsities of his third dimension. His eventual awareness becomes the path away from the ego and the third dimensional world to the path of ascension into the higher vibrational spiritual realms.

Because the incarnate life is truly an illusion, much like a holographic reflective exercise based on the Soul's authentic script and prescribed drama, the Soul constantly reminds the incarnate of the ultimate truth and gives the incarnate constant encouragement and direction in making the Soul's decisions and relegating the ego as an often bothersome, distracting, and separating force to tempt the incarnate in seeking only the egos needs and desires.

Man's ego is the opaque barrier of separation between spirit and the physical being. As ego develops and becomes more and more entranced with material accumulation, power, and other apparent distracting missions and products of our lives, we become attached to them because they give the ego a constant feeding of gratifying emotions and a constant pursuit of pleasure without consideration of the spiritual consequence. The more we feed the ego, the third dimensional separate self, the more we separate from our Soul, our true being. The lessons that we chose with our Spirit Council come up for us again and again in each lifetime until we find the path of Spirit. It is here, with the Spirit Council, where the gift of choice is provided. The ego, when allowed to be in charge, makes illusionary choices with a relative either/or dilemma. It grapples to stay in charge. It seeks to be continually satisfied. Some people suggest that the ego is the human personification of evil or Satan. While that may not be a truth, it does suggest that the ego, with the emotions, thought, mind, and body in tow, generally has its way—further keeping us in duality and separating us from who we truly are.

This is not to suggest that the ego is all bad. As author *Ken Carey* says in his brilliant book, *The Return of the Bird Tribes;*

> *Your ego is here to look after your physical body, to make sure it gets enough to eat, to make sure it doesn't walk over the edge of a cliff or damage itself unknowingly. Your ego is the steward and potential master of all material-plane fears, an important and necessary component of your identity. However, your ego was never meant to provide you with your primary sense of self. In a healthy state, the ego is a secondary component of identity.*

Carey goes on to say that in a healthy state, the Being behind all Being, the self behind all self, the Great Spirit behind all creation, is experienced as your primary sense of self. Your ego does not have to be repressed or transcended for this to happen. It does not have to die. It simply has to assume an *appropriate relationship* with *the Spirit that in truth you are*, the Spirit that wants to incarnate and take up residence in your body/mind/heart system.

Ego simply needs to be controlled and mitigated by our minds and thoughts. It has a temporary existence and is needed for our bodies to exist in the temporary three-dimensional world. One would not survive to find Spirit without one's ego, yet ego is an inhabitant of the third dimension and because it is trapped in the third dimension it *exists* only as an illusion. The trick is to remove the ego from one's driver's seat and take charge of life without the ego's overwhelming distractions.

So what helps us stop making the same choices in this dimension over and over as our egos demand? What can we do to limit the power of our egos and return from our sense of duality and separateness? What can we do to recognize and be aware of our Oneness?

As the pattern seeking individuals that we are, we more often follow the tendency to revert to our historical patterns of behavior and subsequently choose the same path each time the redundant situation is presented—no matter in how many different forms and guises it may appear over this and other lifetimes. We mentioned earlier that the ego will make choices on this relative plane that tend to keep you from following the course chosen by you in your Spirit Council. There *must* be some modifying voice within us that helps us make the Spirit choices so we can release ourselves from this seemingly perpetual conundrum.

Let's reintroduce the legendary Disney character, *Jiminy Cricket*. You may recall him standing on the shoulder and next to the ear of the wooden boy hero, *Pinocchio, in Disney's movie Pinocchio*. Jiminy was continually giving Pinocchio warnings and moral advice in vain, in opposition to Pinocchio's overwhelming desire to go to the fictional and sinful *Pleasure Island*, the choice of his pleasure-seeking, striving to satisfy the only-feel-good ego. Jiminy Cricket represents the symbolism of the power and guidance of intuition, that inner modifying voice that we hear within but do not always act upon. Intuition is the Jiminy Cricket-like guide that continually advises one to make the right spirit choice. It is the voice from one's own higher self, our authentic self, as founded, reflected, and nurtured in one's Spirit Council in the *space between*. We all have it. We all have a Spirit Council. We all experience its direction. Many of us, of course, ignore it in the quest for the power, blinded by the material pleasure of the ego which, like Pinocchio, constantly seeks its own pleasure and satisfaction—no matter the cost.

Even with the considerable power of the ego's quest, each of us has our intuitive Soul voice within helping us to consider whether the choice the ego is making is the choice of the Soul. Most often, like Pinocchio, we follow the ego. That's why we keep reincarnating into yet another body to be presented with the same dilemmas until we choose the spiritual intent of our Soul. Those who pay attention to their intuition, the voice within, and awaken to Spirit, have tapped into the power of the Soul and find the guidance that assists one in following one's Soul's intent. Your Soul's intent is evident and apparent when one examines it from the perspective of the Spirit Council when you authentically exercised your free will and intention. Being aware, paying attention to one's intuition, to one's inspirations, and paying attention to one's intentions and actions is the key to understanding free will. It is the key to understanding the chasm between duality and Oneness.

---

1. Akashic Record: The etheric records that store attitudes, emotions, and concepts from the mental mind as the physical body experiences tastes, smells, sights, sounds, and thoughts during each incarnation. Files are used to make the experiences in other incarnations regardless of the levels of existence, in earth or in the etheric world.

Awareness — A First Step

Who has the capacity to become aware? The short and correct answer is that we all have the capacity to do so. Some, however, seem to be closer to becoming aware than others. Are they more advanced Souls? No, the ability to become aware has nothing to do with the relative level of one's Soul. All Souls are on the same path. One's readiness is determined by a myriad of factors and cosmic invitations, some of which are described below. Becoming aware could be a long and seemingly eternal process or it can occur instantaneously by a meaningful or intuitive joyful event.

We live in the three-dimensional world of duality. We see ourselves as separate from one another and we separate ourselves from our Spirit by believing that life begins and ends with the physical body. In truth, with this kind of thinking, we are separated from our Spirit, our God. This separation began eons ago when man became so entranced with the physical and material world that he forgot his origins. The Christians refer to this as *"The fall from Grace."*. Symbolically, Adam and Eve were forced to leave the Garden because they became so enamored and attached to the fruits of the material world. Because of this continued pandering to our own egos and the physical, material world, and our "forgetfulness" of who we truly are, the vast majority of we humans live in a separate reality from the truth.

Because we believe and accept separate individualism as the reality that is presented to us in this the third dimension, we have separated ourselves from Truth, from God. We have forgotten who we really are in the mad rush to attachments and the illusions of the material world. Our mission, our purpose, in these lifetimes, is to return to who we really are. A return to Love. A return to God. That has always been our deepest heart's desire, the intent of our soul, our purpose.

The truth is that we are all one. We are all part of one another. We are all connected together and one with God. We are God. All of us—together. Science has demonstrated that we all consist of the same substances, molecules, atoms, and space. That includes everything—you, me, animals, rocks, vegetation—everything. How we vibrate determines our relationship with one another. Our vibration determines our place in the universe.

Most of us are puzzled as to how to begin this journey inward. We have to start with the understanding of who we truly are. That first step in that spiritual sojourn is to *Awareness*. It is the initial move toward understanding who you truly are.

To become AWARE is to realize that you are much more than your physical body and mind and that the AUTHENTIC you resides simultaneously in another dimension

The physical body in which one resides is but a *projection* of one's Spirit and is, actually, an illusion. AWARENESS *begins with the recognition of the truth that this physical being is a conditioned and impermanent state.*

Awareness can come about by many means: inspiration, intuition, intellectual consideration, dreams, near-death experiences, physical experiences, mental exercise, books, spiritual leaders, suggestion, teachers, despair, joyousness and many other non-obvious invitations.

Once one is aware, there is *a major shift in perspective* from wallowing around in the intellectual and material third dimensional world with little or no spiritual influence—to initiating and paying attention to and opening one's mind to the reality of our simultaneous existence in other dimensions. When one is aware, one recognizes and embraces one's spirituality. Awareness suggests a shift from thinking exclusively only within the third dimension to the awareness that we live in *multiple* dimensions—all in the same moment. *It is this shift in perspective that opens a path to realizing that you are much more than this physical body* and the world around you is *not* where you truly reside.

Intuition, Trust & Inspiration

One's chief ally in this quest is one's own *intuition and inspiration*. Intuition is the small, almost inaudible voice from within that comes when one is in a state of inspired awareness. It is always there—just like Pinocchio's Jiminy Cricket—even when we choose not to pay attention to its quiet yet persistent voice. Intuition is the Spirit guide and teacher from within that is in touch with one's multiple dimensions. When we realize our intuition and listen to and follow it, we are able to live a life on earth that prepares us for the next level of existence.

As Paramahansa Yogananda said,

> *Intuition is soul guidance, appearing naturally within us during those instants when one's mind is calm. The goal of contemplation is to calm the mind, that without distortion it may hear the infallible counsel of the Inner Voice.*

Intuition is born neither of thoughts from the mind or of the brain, but is birthed from the vast *knowingness* of one's Soul—one's true being. This knowingness is to be followed by embarking on a mindful inquiry as to the merits of the potential inner truth of the intuition or inspiration. Life experiences that have given a preponderance of evidence to us seem to display strong indications of the truth, but we must realize that any truth born in the third dimension is always suspect. Differing apparent truths will appear at different dimensional and vibrational levels.

A third dimensional truth is subject to modification when, for instance, another sentient being can demonstrate that such an accepted truth is not fully a universal truth. For example, we generally all feel the weight of a supposed truth that postulates that if one puts one's hand in a fire, the result will be a painful experience that may well lead to a physical injury and result in the long-term scarring of the area burned. However, as we have seen demonstrated by some yogis, sages, and other mystics, they may allegedly accept the burn yet suffer no ill effects from the fire. If this is so, then the generally accepted truth is surely subject to modification, if not outright rejection. Perhaps the sentient being demonstrating such behavior obviates the generally accepted truth while demonstrating a more universal truth. Truth is thus shown to be a relative state of illusion in the third dimension and can only truly exist in yet another dimension of which one may not as yet be aware. Kahlil Gibran wisely cautions us,

> *Never say I have found **the** truth, but rather say, I have found **A** truth.*

Trust is another significant step in the growing process. In order to reprogram our thoughts and begin to separate belief from truth, one must begin the process of changing one's perspective and trust the inner voice of intuition. Truth is not conditioned but arises in the moment, in the Now. There is an old adage, *Change your thoughts, Change your life.* One may not initially be able to easily trust that as truth, not after so many lives living a dualistic existence.

One can, however, begin one's quest by opening to something more easily assimilated. Let's call it *experimental faith*. One knows instinctively that one's Soul exists, even as centuries of ego driven actions have suggested otherwise. Experimental faith is the act of accepting the possibility that there is more than life in the third dimension. One has to practice that faith, experiment with it and demonstrate it in one's daily sojourns. Try experimental faith for an extended period of time. You will be guided by your awareness and intuition. You are *never* on the wrong path. You are on the path you have chosen, albeit emanating from you in another dimension. Experimental faith gives you permission to explore your spirituality. From that permission you will generate the strength of trust. From trust will flow a cascade of new and exciting spiritual opportunities leading to a symphony of methods of inquiry opening the doors to enlightenment. When one opens to alignment with one's spiritual purpose, one opens to joy and one will become immersed in the process of ascension.

The Purposeful Inquiry

After awareness, alignment, and attention to your intuition comes the process of *inquiry*. Inquiring as to your spiritual purpose and practices can manifest in many forms. Perhaps the simplest, yet most effective practice is meditation. When the mind is stilled in meditation, one is open to be downloaded with intuitive and spiritual direction.

As the ancient sage, Chuang Tsu said,

> *When we become interested in meditation, it is a sign that we are ready to take the journey to another level.*

As long as the journey remains an outer one, the real goal of our endeavors is never in sight. We continue looking out there for our destination, never realizing that the "I" that is doing the looking is what we are actually looking for.

Begin by sitting in silence using any method that is acceptable to you. In the beginning make it a short session as you get used to the new routine. Five or ten minutes a day to start is a solid foundation to launch your inquiry. It may be helpful to use a meditation timer. Eventually, as you become comfortable with the commitment, lengthen the time spent, increasing in increments of five or ten minutes, until you are sitting a half hour to an hour a day in meditative silence.

Do your best to carve out a time period wherein you have little or no distractions. The wee hours of the morning are often known as *God's Hours*. If you are able to designate an early morning discipline for meditation, your day becomes more fulfilling as you will enter each day with a calm and quiet perspective. However, any time that is convenient is a good time. Keeping to a schedule is part of training the mind. The mind comes to expect and look forward to it. You may view this time as *keeping an appointment with God*. It is most effective when you have a set time where you bathe in the silence and your active thoughts can be dissipated. Late in the evening after all the hustle and bustle of the day has been suppressed and any family or entertainment distractions are completed, can also work well.

Meditation can also be spontaneous and unscheduled. When one is going through the various activities of one's day, there are always moments when one can drift calmly into a meditative state by connecting with whatever one is doing fully in the present. When one does so, one's autonomic system takes over and performs the physical functions that life brings and demands. Activities such as gardening, washing family dishes, sitting in contemplation, gazing at a wondrous flower, bird, insect, the sky, ocean, river or lake— or even driving one's car can offer moments for meditation opportunities. Take every possible opportunity to silence and calm one's monkey mind that tends through conditioning to swing from thought to thought.

Your inquiry may also include your study of ancient spiritual texts such as the Tao de Ching, the Upanishads, the Vedas, the Bible, Koran and Bhagavad-Gita. There are a myriad of books and articles written by sages and fellow seekers that present a host of ideas and experiences that may well attract one to purposeful thought and intuition.

Talking circles wherein one exchanges thoughts, opinions, prayers and writings can be very supportive, especially if one approaches such activities as an inquirer rather than as a critic. Any spiritual conversation about rituals or interpreting puzzling passages written in spiritual texts, can be helpful, again if it is for inquiry rather than criticism or judgment. One may not always agree with another's path and practice, but there is always the opportunity for appreciation and respect for such alleged differences.

Of course, there can, and usually will be, the appearance of teachers. A teacher may reveal itself in many guises. One normally can recall sayings and writings of well-known sages, ascended master beings, poets, gurus, priests, and ministers. Their thoughts are often catalysts to spiritual inquiry. One, however, should never discount a seemingly innocuous and casual conversation or incident with another sentient being, human or otherwise, that reveals to you a truth that arches over a belief. Every being one meets is a *holy encounter* capable of bringing to one a truth or nugget of wisdom that can launch personal missiles of aspirations that may ignite a connection within. As the Course in Miracles says,

> *When you meet anyone, remember it is a holy encounter.*
> *As you see him you will see yourself.*
> *As you treat him you will treat yourself.*
> *As you think of him you will think of yourself.*
> *Never forget this, for in him you will find yourself or lose yourself.*

A wonderful way of tuning one's physical mind, brain and body to pursue and appreciate a spiritual path each day is to begin the day with an affirmation of joy. Upon first waking, demonstrate to your mind that the *authentic you* is in charge by setting the tone for the joyfulness that can be realized in the blossoming day. A simple affirming thought that reminds you that the day will be wonderful and joyous, and that you will strive to weather any psychological storm that may arise, will point the mind towards joyfulness. This will be a loving and powerful launching pad for one's journey of inquiry and awareness.

One may also shift one's attention from conflicting personal stimuli and judgment to episodes of tolerance and finally to the holy acceptance of *what is* through appreciation. Appreciation becomes the antithesis of judgment. At the end of one's day, a satisfying culminating activity is to run the *movie of one's day* through your mind and note the areas of love, forgiveness, and challenges one has encountered. And, as one drifts off to slumber, the warm thoughts of the day's affirming actions, whether physical or mental, guides one into the pleasant dreams that can be the vanguard of your morning thoughts.

Practice & Manifestation

After having investigated the many methods of inquiry and having begun a protracted practice of meditation, discipline and commitment, the joyful practice of one's methodology becomes the dominant feature of the journey. It is in this realm where the *Law of Attraction* firmly asserts itself. One begins to recognize how one's thoughts ignite and propel that law; which simply states that what one concentrates on, what one gives attention to, what one launches as explosive desire, will be activated to bear fruit. What one holds energetically in the deepest recesses of one's being, is what one will receive. When one attunes to the vibration of love, forgiveness, abundance, compassion, surrender, and gratitude, the Law of Attraction will manifest these qualities in one's life. Conversely, when one dwells in the house of negativity, the Law of Attraction will bring those experiences instead. It is up to you to determine what you choose to invite and activate, love or fear—unity consciousness or the consciousness of separation.

Even as one seems settled into a quiet, comfortable spiritual routine, one will intuit and find that new insights enter one's fixed discipline and invite one to modify or adjust one's system of beliefs and truths. This is natural. Consider it a gift from the authentic self urging one to sophisticate one's regaled practices. Remember that truth has a different vision and quality at differing levels of existence and vibration. All practices that connect one with Source are correct practices when they are replete with love, forgiveness, compassion, gratitude, and abundance for all. The lesson here is to be open to the righteous voice of one's authentic self.

To manifest is to make real. Such a definition becomes cloudy unless one sees that manifestation is not simply physical power, control, thought, or material wants. The foundation of *real* depends upon one's vibration in the cosmic universe. The Law of Attraction guarantees a vibration of existence in alignment with what one chooses to attract in this dimension.

A connection with your authentic self in a higher dimension, rather than accepting the third dimensional illusion, is a major part of one's daily quest. What may seem to be *real* in this, the third dimension, may not exhibit reality at all in the higher realms. As we operate in our relative world, the world of black and white, good and evil, up and down, as well as the myriads of other relative concepts that we embrace in this dimension, we tend to forget that such perceived realities are actually illusions. One has to remember that those relative concepts are illusory *because this third dimension is not one's authentic self.* The third dimension is simply a manifested illusion propagated by time and one's ego, replete with authentic hints of a reflection and construct of your authentic self—the preprogramming that occurred in the aforementioned *space between.*

As one becomes more adept in actuating the directions of one's authentic being, that is listening to and following the intuition from your *authentic* being, one's ability to manifest becomes more instantaneous. One's illusionary self in the third dimension may still experience manifestation, but such manifestation includes more attentiveness to the authentic self's messages through awareness, intuition, and practice. Once one attains that connective awareness, manifestation of dualistic material power or circumstance is no longer desired. Connection with authentic spirit becomes paramount.

Truth and Belief

Are we able to determine what truth is? Or more commonly, what constitutes a belief? Specifically, can one determine what is one's truth or one's belief? What is the difference between truth and belief? Are we able to separate the two? Is truth or belief a local, personalized issue that relates to a particular time and circumstance or is it a universal principle that can be applied at all levels? Can there be differing levels of truth?

We trundle through life believing concepts and perceptions we consider to be truths. Why? Because we have grown up with them and most of the folks around us accept them as truths. We choose to accept these beliefs because we have been taught through our ingrained historical customs, our elders, or by one's religious training, that they are, indeed, truths. We accept those concepts without much internal critique—perhaps without any spiritual inquiry. Not believing these commonly accepted concepts may isolate or perhaps ostracize one from family, one's friends, community, or nation. Beliefs seem to sustain us and ground us in our daily lives. They provide us with comfort, or so it appears, to live without controversy or conflict with our neighboring third dimensional brethren. When we unilaterally declare a belief, does it suggest that we are released from the consideration that it might be false? Do we therefore become comfortable with such beliefs as truth even though those so called beliefs/truths may not reflect universal or cosmic truth?

Belief continues to present itself as truth until we actively choose to examine it critically—and from within. Upon examination, one's belief may not necessarily prove to be a truth, but rather a simple convenient and semi-permanent mental concept that has been locked away in our mental storage bins where we don't choose to consider it further. If we lock away our perceived truths, we can conveniently "get on with life's other seemingly important issues." If this is the case, then we are living an illusion, a false truth, and a belief—a witting lie disguised as a truth that keeps us from looking for authentic or universal truth.

This is not to imply that belief itself is necessarily an exclusively simple illusion. Any perception that originates in the mind can manifest itself to what we perceive to be *real*. Those perceptions represent our thoughts and our thoughts create our world. Thus, our world, our perceptions, as we create them, becomes our reality. But is that perceived reality the truth, or is it simply a belief stored away as an illusionary truth? Is it true that we only exist in this third dimension? Or are we even capable of answering the question? Where, indeed, do we truly exist? We learn that as we shift our awareness of our vibrational selves to higher levels of vibration, i.e. our true reality, our authentic self in a higher dimension, our awareness heightens and we begin to unveil truth and separate it from mere belief.

We learn that true universal reality is a manifested vibration that connects us with the dimension wherein we truly exist. Our moment to moment, day to day, emotional responses set the stage for drawing life experiences to us. The eternal Law of Attraction determines how we manifest those thoughts and beliefs. Belief is not just thought. It is a quality of vibration. We are, after all, vibrational beings. Our vibrations are manifest in this third dimension by how we think. What we think is what we are and what we create. Again, the Law of Attraction assists in this manifestation.

Nonetheless, in this third dimension of existence where the mass majority of us cavort, we recognize and identify our perceived realities based on our poorly tested beliefs rather than truths. We thus continue to confer our truth, shrouded by our beliefs, to the limited third dimension.

We have accumulated an impressive body of beliefs. We can believe the world is beautiful—or not beautiful—our choice. And according to our perceptions, we may believe that we are either smart or, perhaps, even naïve or stupid. We believe in good or evil. Our daily lives in this third dimension showcase good and evil in many forms. We further believe that we were created by an almighty and omnipotent God, and many of us have created and engendered another set of complicated beliefs to support that premise. We continue to accept, create, and practice such beliefs convincing ourselves that our beliefs are truths. And if we continue to believe these as truth, it will remain true for us and as such, we will continue to define our realities by our beliefs. And those beliefs will remain our predominant truths even as they may simply reflect our comfortable feelings in a consensus reality.

Human Beings are pattern seeking entities. Guided by the ego, we look for patterns that confirm our attachment to such beliefs and these attachments to beliefs are apparent everywhere. In order to step away from our standard beliefs, we need to challenge those common mental concepts, forever seeking truth. For example, historically, we as a species once believed that the earth was flat. That was comfortable at the time as the vast majority of mankind believed it to be flat. Those who didn't conform to that common belief were looked upon as crackpots, crazies, or scary alchemists. It took centuries to test that belief and disprove it by examination, study, and experience. I'm sure each of us can list a myriad of one's early beliefs that have since proved false when examined in a different light, in a different place or a different time.

So what can we define and know to be a truth, and not simply a belief? This is a difficult question because there are so many, many, beliefs that we have long and falsely considered to be truths. To begin questioning all of our beliefs at once would conjure in our minds an almost insurmountable and daunting task and we could abandon the entire process in frustration. No matter how seemingly enormous or insurmountable the task, however, we must begin the quest. To not do so would be at the very least, neglectful, and at worst, wasting one's life. The basic question of who we are and what our purpose is on this beautiful blue planet is the initial key to understand the foundation of universal truth.

I'm not at all suggesting that such a quest is an easy task! But it is a sojourn we must begin if we are truly going to understand the vast differences between what is truth, belief, or illusion. If we don't begin, then we are programmed to continue the never ending re-circulating cycle of birth and death emanating from fear and illusion. Accordingly, there is no valid reason or cause why one should exit this life with any semblance of fear or illusion.

The search for ourselves and why we are here is the crucial venture we need to undertake. In fact, it is *the most important quest* in our lives. We can, of course, choose not to attempt the seemingly enormous task of separating truth from illusion, and seeming to save ourselves protracted quandaries of mind by simply take life as it comes. One gets to do that. And life will and does come, seemingly chaotically and randomly, always filled with fear, amazement, good stuff and bad stuff. If we don't make this quest for truth, life will seem meaningless at the end of this incarnation. Why spend a life of endurance, fear, and mystery when we are given the unique opportunity to utilize our limited precious time on this earth to discover the basic tenets of our existence and eradicate the residue of fear that permeates our lives? How do we begin such a daunting sojourn?

Let's begin this quest with a discussion of some things that we can recognize as truth from our third dimension and some of the facts that constitute the embodiment of truth, and cease following lemming-like off the spiritual cliff laden with invalid perceptions while maintaining a closet full of potentially illusionary beliefs. Knowing that truth in the third dimension is always suspect, and that levels of truth change in higher dimensions, following are ten truths that can provide a strong foundation for our path out of illusion.

TRUTH #1

We are Eternal Spiritual Beings Temporarily Expressing Through a Physical Body

WE EXIST, *PHYSICALLY,* in a three-dimensional world. We all recognize this as our basic reality and truth. Our spirit, however, the authentic entity, lives above and/or aside this dimension. We use the term *above* or *aside* to delineate the other non-physical dimensions. It is not a lineal demarcation. We actually live in parallel existences. We exist in the past, present and future at the same moment. We are aware and conscious of what we think and the familiar five senses that permeate this 3-D world. As such, we define that sensory experience as what is "real." What we see, hear, touch, smell and taste constitutes our accepted view of reality.

We are generally comfortable with this view of our world because we do not understand, or are unaware of, the limitations we are subjected to with these minimum sentient tools. In truth, this world seems very real because we are viewing it exclusively

with these limited senses.
As Teilhard de Chardin, a noted French scholar said;

> *It is misleading to think that you are a physical being having a spiritual experience. Rather take the view that you are a spiritual being having a worldly experience.*

I can hear silent protests as I share this truth. I realize how foreign this statement may be for many of us because it seems directly opposite to our accepted sense and perception of reality. But it's time for us to literally think out of the traditional three-dimensional confines of our mind.

It follows that if we are spiritual beings in truth, then our current existence in the 3-D world constitutes a false truth, an illusion. We are "penciled" into this illusion for a specified time and because time doesn't, and cannot, exist in the spiritual realm, the fourth and higher dimensions, we have difficulty understanding the freedom of not being a slave to the concept of time. Our true existence is in the infinite world, the spiritual world, not in the 3-D finite world that we frolic in. We are temporary visitors in this world of five senses. We are not aware, or more truthfully, we have *forgotten* who we really are.

Knowing that we are concurrently spiritual beings as well as *temporary* physical beings is not a new concept. Spiritual masters, biblical scholars, and ancient scriptures such as the Upanishads and Vedas have revealed this truth for centuries. All major religions have addressed this in one form or another since the beginning of man's appearance on the planet. The Hindus, Buddhists, Muslims, Native Americans and other major religious sects have practiced ascension with this basic premise as their foundation. We are eternal spiritual beings temporarily living in a physical body.

TRUTH # 2

This is Not our First Appearance in a Physical Form

. . . AND IN ALL LIKELIHOOD, it will not be your last. You have lived countless lives, all of which were chosen by you while in the spiritual realm with the help of your inner Spirits. Ah yes, you heard me right. You chose your life (lives). This is the concept and birthplace of reincarnation.

It is not so remarkable to consider the fact of reincarnation any more that it is/was to be born in the first place. What is remarkable to us is that there is no time in the spiritual realm and therefore no past or future. Here in our Christian oriented western world, we may have forgotten that reincarnation was once a tenet of Christianity. It was forcefully removed through a political act at the Council of Nicea in 553 A.D. when it was ordered stricken from any scriptures during the reign and leadership of Roman Emperor Justinian. Much of the rest of the non-Christian world, in spite of the Christian dictate, has continued the truth and understanding of reincarnation. Latter day Christians, however, have been taught since Nicea to negate this truth because, at the time, the bishops found that it was difficult to control, manipulate and lead people who did not hold the fear of death. And we should not be ignorant regarding early religious organizations, for they understood power. If the fear of death was absent, they opined, the people could not easily be manipulated by the political and religious leaders of those eras.

We reincarnate from one body to another depending on our desires and planning while residing in that "space between" in the Spirit world. Each incarnation is another opportunity for us to address our *Karma*. The law of karma is an ancient Hindu derivative term known as cause and effect in the Western world. It is simply a matter of the old axiom of *what you sew, so shall you reap*. It is the Law of Attraction playing out. Life becomes a matter of daily choice to address those karmic debts or rewards that we carry into our next life. Each incarnation brings us the spiritual challenges that we have not completed in our past lives. And now we face those challenges once again, in perhaps a different form, a different place in time, and in our new incarnate state. How we face each chosen challenge determines our path of enlightenment.

During the incarnation we have chosen, we are given *free choice*. That free choice, however, is determined in that *space between* with the guidance of our spiritual mentors and with the proviso that we will *not remember* our past lives or challenges. Non-remembrance is an act of love. With remembrance, our free choice would be wholly limited in making decisions under the actual auspices of free will. This lack of remembrance enables us to choose freely again *without the burden* of knowing the outcome. Knowing the outcome would negate true free choice. Our Spirit Council in the space between has designed the parameters of choice in our experiences. If we choose the tenets of love, emanating from the spirit realm, and practice love, rather than fear, we will pass that challenge and go on to other lessons on our karmic record. If, indeed, we have completed our karmic lessons, we will not need to incarnate again, but will ascend to another dimension void of materiality. If we don't choose love in such lessons, we will return again and again until we overcome ego and fear.

TRUTH # 3

There's Only ONE of Us Here!

YES, YOU READ THAT CORRECTLY. We are not a separate gaggle of individual entities seeking separate ascension or individual demise. We are all ONE! Everything, and I do mean everything—mountains, rivers, flora, fauna, your kitchen table, automobiles, and YOU are part of a grand whole. All that I have mentioned and more consists of three things: space, molecules and atoms. Atoms, in turn are made up of sub-atomic particles known as protons, electrons and neutrons which constitute the contents of *everything* in the universe. All of these sub-atomic particles are packets of energy. These "packets of energy" are the "stuff" of the universe. Sub-atomic particles are not made up of energy—they ARE energy. How they are arranged is a result of their vibrations. And, according to quantum physics, they exist because of our observation.

What that means is that when we look at and observe something, it contains *potential*. It manifests not necessarily as what we would perceive as a particle, perhaps commensurate to a grain of sand, but also as a *wave*. That means that *how* we observe something gives it the form we are drawing into being. We, as third dimensional beings, thus create, or co-create with our Source, what the particle or wave does in the world we live in. Quantum physics also suggests the existence of parallel universes, parallel lives, objects being in two or more places at the same time, and baffling consequences of movement that are devoid of speed or traditional concepts of existence. Even the discoverers of quantum physics initially refused to believe the phenomenon. Consequently, a long held *belief* had been discovered to be incomplete or false, and a new truth was uncovered.

A clearer example of wholeness or Oneness rather than that of separateness can be demonstrated by examining the structure of our own human body. We are each made up of trillions of individual cells. Each cell is, in fact, an independent single organism acting in concert with all the other cells in the body to form what we identify to be a human being, each part working seemingly independently, but actually a cooperative, integral and necessary part of the whole body. That is the essence of Oneness. It takes just a little more imagination and perception to extrapolate Oneness into a complex combination of human bodies working cooperatively together to fulfill the existence and function of yet a *higher* being. That extrapolation can further extend and conform to the function of yet an even higher being or entity—and eventually, to our Source, to God. A fundamental truth is, indeed, *We Are All One*. We are all comprised of the same material and we are all interconnected to form a single whole.

TRUTH # 4

There are only Two Emotions on our Third Dimensional Plane, Love and Fear

B UT THEY ARE NOT OPPOSITES as Love can have no opposition and contains *all that is*. Love is equal to expansion while fear equates with contraction. Love is not the simple third dimensional definition that we generally embrace. While our traditional definition seems to serve us in this dimension, what we understand as love is simply a small and ego-driven part of the whole dimension of love.

J. Krishnamurti, a 20th century spiritual sage, had this to say about love.

> *The highest form of sensitivity with the brain—completely still—is the quality of love. Love is a most extraordinary thing if you have it in your heart. Love is not pleasure. Love has nothing to do with fear. It is not related to sex. It is the quality of the mind*

that is free, sensitive, and intelligent with the brain not responding in terms of the past . . therefore, still. Then the heart comes upon this perfume called love. The understanding of that is meditation. That is the foundation of meditation.

Love has a universal spiritual aspect that transcends our limited view of the term. It is not love between individuals or loved ones, although those feelings are appropriate in our familiar dimension. Love is a grander term, an acceptance and embracing of loving *what is* rather than what one wishes it to be.

The highest form of love is to love universally and unconditionally, without depending upon or expecting anything in return. When one gives universal and unconditional love, one is giving to the universe, not to a person or object. That which one loves comes and goes, but the capacity to love is eternal and will never disappear.

Universal love contributes to one's connection with the Divine. There is an axiom in spiritual transcending that is known as *surrender*. The Webster Dictionary definition of surrender is *giving up*. In the context of our third dimension, giving up connotes failure, and failure is something we traditionally seek to avoid. However, in the spiritual concept, surrender means to give oneself over to something bigger than oneself, to a universe that knows what it is doing. Expanding to a more generous definition, surrender means giving up all attachment to results and letting go of the concept of *me*. When we surrender to our higher self, we release our attachment as to how things should happen to us in the outer world and become more aware of what happens in our inner world. If we realize that our authentic experience is to love—which is our true purpose—we release our need to control expectations for the outcome.

When we maintain attachment to results, we have a difficult time giving up control. The true joy in surrender is being able to relax and feel the love in one's heart. One then can choose to keep love as one's focus in every moment or situation and experience the true meaning of spiritual surrender. When one surrenders to a greater power and purpose, an amazing phenomenon occurs—our perception and experience of the world changes. The world softens when we choose to surrender. We are not giving up, as some would suggest, but we are accepting that we are not in control and allowing a higher power to guide and help us in each moment.

Wayne Dyer, noted author, teacher, and lecturer has this reminder hanging on his wall next to his bed.

Good Morning, This is God. I will be handling all of your problems today. I will not need your help, so have a miraculous day!

What a wonderful example of spiritual surrender!

Perhaps my favorite guiding principle of love and fear comes from *Marianne Williamson,* in her first book, *Return to Love.* In her poignant discussions of love and fear which are based on *A Course in Miracles*, she describes our intended purpose here on this planet.

We are all assigned a piece of the garden, a corner of the universe that is ours to transform. Our corner of the universe is our own life—our relationships, our homes, our work—our current circumstances exactly as they are.

Every situation we find ourselves in is an opportunity, perfectly planned by Divine Spirit, to teach love instead of fear.

One changes from within when one embraces love instead of fear. *A Course in Miracles* says that one who is focused on love will experience a state of atonement, defined as the correction of our perceptions.

TRUTH # 5

There is Only NOW

PERHAPS THE MOST OBVIOUS, yet unrecognized element in one's life is, *Now*. We use the term in many contexts, but we have not fully understood the significance and power of either the word or its meaning. Now is this moment. Now will be the next moment—in the next moment. We often relate it to time, but it is actually timeless. The only infinite moment we experience in this third dimension is Now. It is instantaneous and it occurs outside of time. Now is the only reality. All else is a fabrication of mind.

In the present moment, there is no past and no future. There is only *NOW*. I repeat; in Now there is no such element as time. As author, *Gina Lake*, noted in her book, *Embracing the Now;*

The present moment, the Now, is where we meet our true self…when we aren't involved with the egoic mind, we move into the Now and the experience of who we really are.

When one considers the element of time, one wiles oneself in the past and the future. Such cavorting in time challenges one to continually accept the path of the ego and not seek what is beyond. After all, we as human beings continually seek those old familiar and misguided patterns. Such is our programmed nature. However, as quoted in *A Course in Miracles*,

> *The wheels of time are mysterious. Time is a concept of the mind. Without mind, there is no concept of time. Annihilate the mind. You will go beyond time. You will enter the realm of timeless. You will live in the eternal. Now is the closest approximation of eternity that this world offers. It is in the reality of NOW, without past or future that the beginning of the appreciation of eternity lies. For only NOW is here. To be born again is to let the past go, and look without condemnation upon the present.*

Wow, what a realization! The beginning of the appreciation of eternity lies in *Now*. How does that happen? How does one recognize and embrace Now?

When one finally stills the mind, one lives with eternity. This stilling of the mind can occur in the process of meditation when we have the brain and mind in submissive status to the super consciousness of Spirit. This is why we meditate, to be aware in the moment, to be aware in *Now*. This expansiveness can also exist at any instant when one is tuned into and is aware of one's vibrational frequency in the present moment. Past and future quickly becomes recognized as excess baggage that clouds the pureness of Now and serves to hold us in the limited third dimension of relativity. In Now we become alert and aware of our vibrational transmitters and receivers. Our spiritual antennas are primed in the direction of Source and we are instruments of transmission and reception. We become in touch with our authentic spiritual intuition, inspiration, and Love and learn to bask in the sanctity of Oneness.

As Eckert Tolle, who tirelessly points us to this Truth, says,

Transform your life by the simple realization that the only time you ever have is this moment. To offer no resistance to life is to be in a state of grace, ease, and lightness. This state is then no longer dependent upon things being in a certain way, good or bad. It seems paradoxical, yet when your inner dependency on form is gone, the general conditions of your life, the outer forms, tend to improve greatly.

Our civilization is built on the achievements of the mind, and many are remarkable. We naturally opt to confuse the mind, in its constantly thinking state, as being Us. However, there is a being-ness behind the mind that is the real I; by getting in tune with it, we can control our thoughts and put our emotions into perspective. Until we control our mind, it controls us.

It becomes a lesson in true consciousness to embrace *Now*. *Now* asks us to be more present in the minutiae of everyday life, to see if one can make every moment mean something. Some forms of mental illness involve an inability to shut off internal conversations. In contrast, someone in the fullest mental health will have the ability to quiet the mind, and from this stillness access the true state of Being.

TRUTH # 6

Life Proceeds According to our Intention for it!

THERE IS A CLASSIC AND accepted definition of intent that appears in most dictionaries as follows:

A strong purpose or aim, accompanied by a determination to produce a desired result.

A more spiritual definition might be as author Carlos Castaneda suggested;

Intent is a force that exists in the universe. When Sorcerers (those who live of the Source) beckon intent, it comes to them and sets up the path for attainment, which means that sorcerers always accomplish what they set out to do.

He went on to say,

> *In the universe there is an immeasurable, indescribable force which shamans call intent, and absolutely everything that exists in the entire cosmos is attached to intent by a connecting link.*

Can one fathom that? Intent is not something one *does*, but exists in the universe as an invisible and accessible field of energy.

First there is *intent*, then *desire*, then *will*, which are followed by *manifestation*. One, therefore, *must* pay attention to one's intentions! From one's intentions (germinated from your higher Spirit Council) comes a desire which activates the Law of Attraction. This progression of intent and desire, followed by one's will to manifest desire, results in manifestation. The slower speed of manifestation that exists on the three-dimensional plane is tempered by resistance, patience, and one's vibration. When one affirms something, one affirms it as if it has already happened. Why? Because it is already so and all one has to do is remove one's resistance, align with one's vibration, and get the ego out of the way for it to manifest.

As the old axiom suggests, *If you don't like what you have chosen, choose again.* Life proceeds out of one's intention for it. One cannot change the past because it is forever gone. Living in the past forces one to revisit and sustain a finished story. It is over. Trying to change the past is a futile and distracting chore. It behooves us to begin in this moment to live with joyful intention and witness how the law of attraction changes circumstances.

Whatever one puts one's attention to gets energy and grows. Remove the attention and it dies. One must be conscious and deliberate in this. Intention always goes along with attention. What one intends and gives attention to begins to manifest. There are no idle thoughts. One thus becomes what one thinks about. We are the sum total of our thoughts. Matter that has been manifested is merely materialized thought germinated by what we intend and pay attention to.

One may create future outcomes by one's intentions and desires. But it is imperative that one accepts the present moment as *what is*. That moment is Now. The present moment is the perfect outcome of your past thoughts, states and actions. It is a gift that enables one to experience oneself and grow. Resisting and cursing the present only perpetuates its unsatisfactory nature.

We are intentional beings able to craft our lives and co-create with our source. If one lives one's life by what one intends, one has dominion over that which one becomes. This is the secret of intentional being. The roadmap to intentional living is paved with one's emotions. There are aspects of emotion that we can control, if we so choose. One of those aspects is to allow one to vibrate with happiness or grief. When we choose grief, we choose preoccupation with the ego's quest for attention and control. Happiness is also a choice. When we choose happiness, to be happy and powerful, we assign the ego to the passenger seat and open our hearts to the joy of living and seeing and seeking our purpose. Our intent is to live empowered by joy, love, and appreciation. This expansiveness is the freedom that we all seek—the freedom to be our true selves exercising our true knowledge and remembering our complete spirit.

TRUTH # 7

You Must be Selfish Enough to Align with Well-being

SELFISH IS A WORD THAT we generally associate with a negative connotation. No one, it seems, wants to be termed as a selfish being. It sets us apart from our neighbors and is generally frowned upon by general society as are the companion labels of arrogance and conceit.

We need to re-examine such a perspective as it relates to our spiritual initiative. Each of us has our own spiritual path. Each of us has a path that is unique and apropos to one's self, specifically, while operating as a third dimensional creature and aligning with our authentic self. Our path as it is presently constituted is the path that is best for us. It may or may not coincide with the path of others in our physical presence, our neighborhood, or our spiritual circle. Our path may seem somewhat parallel to that of others, especially those with whom we share our innermost thoughts, prayers and meditation. The caution is to not sell one's Soul to the most powerful orator or teacher one encounters but to draw inspiration from many sources, many teachers, because everything is oneself showing to oneself and the challenge is to take responsibility of one's own growth. But make no mistake about it. Your path is your own, not necessarily the way of others.

Because of the personal nature of one's path, it is important not to co-opt one's path by blindly following the path of another. We must not act as lemmings and follow any purported spiritual leader over a cosmic cliff. Yet it is essential to listen to the teachings others are presenting. In most cases they will present to you a spiritual nugget or two that registers in the wisdom category for your own way. Others have their own path and may exhibit many wise elements of the path you are following. But it is not *your* specific path. One must remember that each of us residing on this and other realms and planets is on an inexorable path of ascension. While many of us will cling to some others along the way—perhaps until one reinforces one's own spiritual legs—assuming someone else knows the way—there is truly only your path. And yes, of course, all paths lead to the spiritual summit. But each of us has our own karma and choices and signposts to adhere to along the way. We must never sacrifice our ability to choose from the guidance of our own intuition.

That's what we mean by being selfish. One must follow the path of one's intuition and well-being and not be co-opted by what others think or do, or the flavor of the moment, even as those flavors may bring occasional and meaningful wise council.

Aligning with our own well-being is an important component of our unique path. When one is aligned with well-being, one is on the highway to heaven while here on earth. This becomes an enabling technique of living that opens one's Spirit without the clutter of the mundane illusions that comprise the third dimensional world.

TRUTH # 8

The Law of Attraction is the Most Powerful Law in the Universe

THE LAW OF ATTRACTION IS the magnetic power of the universe that draws similar energies together. It manifests through the power of creation, everywhere and in multiple ways. It manifests through one's thoughts by drawing to one's thoughts and ideas of a similar kind. It is the law and power that brings together people of similar interests and unites them into special groups. It is the most powerful law of the universe and it is in one's individual power to access.

Every thought that one thinks is vibrating at a very personal frequency and attracts other thoughts that are its vibrational match. As a result, those combined thoughts will vibrate at a frequency that is higher than the thought that came before. That combination of thought will then attract another and another and another, until eventually the thoughts will be powerful enough to attract a third-dimensional situation or manifestation.

When one begins to understand the Law of Attraction and

understand that like attracts like, then it becomes easier and easier to understand that one is offering a signal, and the entire universe is responding and one begins to exercise some deliberate control over the signal one offers. Then one will recognize that nothing truly happens outside of one's creative control; nothing happens by chance or circumstance. We are all subject to the law of attraction. What we intend, we attract. It is critical to pay attention to our intentions. Why? Because what we think is what we create. We choose our thoughts. Our thoughts are who we are. Our thoughts are reflective of our intentions. Therefore, what we choose to think is who we are. It's the Law of Attraction.

The Law of Attraction reflects not what one was born into, but what one is, right now. People attract what they are, not necessarily what they think they want. They attract what they love and what they fear, the only two true emotions or orientations of being that exist in the universe.

Take some time to envision and imagine every aspect of your life, as you would like it to be. Your life is outpicturings or projections by your mind, expressed to the extent that they are held in mind and focused on given energy. In this process of introspection, one tends to reexamine one's belief system and begin a journey to attract love and joy.

TRUTH # 9

Happiness Arises through Meditation and Prayer

MEDITATION AND PRAYER ARE POWERFUL communication tools. Prayer gives one the opportunity to talk with God, while meditation gives God the opportunity to talk to us. Both forms of communication usually occur in silence, although prayer often is spoken aloud. Meditation requires a retreat from the consciousness of the mind and a clearing of thought so one may hear the guidance from Source.

Both forms of communication—prayer and meditation—are necessary in order for one to receive one's joy and happiness and eliminate or minimize the ego's insatiable demands of satisfaction.

Perhaps the most useful positive prayer is one of *gratitude*. The historical Roman Emperor, Cicero, had this to say about gratitude.

> *Gratitude is not only the greatest of virtues, but the parent of all the others.*

Prayer has been defined in some quarters as an anguished cry of the soul in distress or helplessness, to a Power fuller and greater than itself, for relief and comfort. It is considered an invocation to God, a source competent enough to grant solace and peace to a mind tortured by the problems of life and life's surroundings. Yes, prayer often is offered during a time of stress and fear. Those are the prayers of anguish. It is usually for the immediate relief of a tortuous situation. Those prayers are surely heard.

A true universal prayer is, indeed, one of gratitude. It is, perhaps, the most useful positive prayer. Annie Elizabeth, in her book, *Affirmations for Everyday Living*, put it this way:

Gratitude is a way of expressing your application of the Universal Mind, sending a message of what it is you would like to have more of in life.

Gratitude is having the vision and grace to accept what is and count our blessings. It is an effective prayer that should always be held in mind.

Are there other worthy prayers? Yes, of course. We regularly pray for others. The main attribute for an effective prayer is that you have already recognized *that what is, is*. The act for which you pray is already proceeding by divine guidance, although it may not be in the direction that you think you wish to experience. The job is to align one's particular vibration with that for which or whom you pray. This will depend on one's ability to accept *what is* and face *what is* with joy. The power of prayer is so profound, yet we must intrinsically know that when they are offered, prayers are answered for *the highest possible good*. We are not always able to consciously agree or know what the highest possible good from a third dimensional conscious level may be. We must be open to listening with our hearts and trust the Divine. One might remember the old axiom, *Man proposes, God disposes.* This is best done by quieting the mind in meditation. Following is a suggested method to practice.

A Suggested Meditative Journey of Light

Find a quiet, comfortable setting where you will not be disturbed by the distractions of your daily routines. Uncross your legs and keep your back straight with hands on your lap sitting in a comfortable pose. Close your eyes and fix your inner gaze forward.

Take this moment and relax your body and mind. Take, slowly, three deep breaths breathing in from your nose, exhaling completely from your mouth until you have purged all the air.

Calm your breathing to normal, or slower.

We are now going to ground ourselves to the mother Gaia-Earth. We will start from our 8th Chakra, the energy-aura space outside your body and just above your head.

Visualize there a warm liquid, white light energy slowly flowing downward over and through your body while relaxing each of your organs, limbs and skin as it begins its journey throughout the body (Go slowly through your entire body, seeing and naming each of its parts.)

As the energy of light touches your entire being and reaches your toes, let it continue its journey, at the speed of thought, deep to the center of the Gaia-mother earth.

When you reach the center of the earth, let it ground you to the mother source.

The energy is bright, plentiful, and warm.

The energy, while still secured to the grounding, begins an ascent back to the body and touches and alerts each of your chakra energy centers showing its colors in ascending order as it passes through each chakra. It begins with red and continues through orange, yellow, green, blue, indigo and then it reaches the violet color of the 7th crown chakra, at the crown of your head.

It is here where you may talk to God through prayer. It is here where we give gratitude for the blessings we have received in this life and past existences. It is here where you ask for your preferences in prayer so you may set your desires in motion for attraction.

One has now talked with God

Let us now ascend up to our 8th chakra, from where we started our journey of light. It is here where God has the opportunity to talk to us while we are paying attention.

It is now time to quietly pay attention and leave all thought below for the next 20 minutes or so.

TRUTH # 10

You Are on the Correct Path

EVERY SOUL TRAVELS ITS OWN path as a glorious and unique aspect of the One Soul. There is no one correct path. Every path leads to the spiritual summit, although some will wind through circuitous routes. No path is exactly the same, yet each path will lead to the same destination—a reunion with one's authentic self with an invitation to ascend into higher dimensions. The physical plane may be the bottom rung on the spiritual ladder, yet it is intrinsically connected with one's Source or God. One may travel on many planes and pathways at the same instant, as we are also having Soul experiences in *parallel* (other) universes concurrently. What that means is that the past, present, and future are happening at the same instant—in what is known as *NOW*. We actually live in parallel universes, all at the same time. All of our incarnations exist at the same time. There is no past or future that truly exists from our physical vantage point. While this concept seems virtually impossible to understand with our finite minds, deep inquiry into our authentic self reveals this to be true. When we learn to live in

NOW, we will live in the infinite expression of timelessness. The construct of time exists only in our third dimension. Yes, it is difficult to imagine and it will only be understood in yet another realm of understanding and existence. One's mind, encased in the third dimension, is incapable of comprehending this truth. Rest assured, however, that this truth will be revealed as one continues one's ascension.

Remember, as *A Course in Miracles* states,

> *The journey to God is merely the reawakening of the knowledge of where you are always, and what you are forever. It is a journey without distance to a goal that has never changed.*

The Native Americans always seem to have a saying that relates directly to our collective pathways. The following is a beautiful lesson from an unknown native source;

> *If we look at the path, we do not see the sky. We are earth people on a spiritual journey to the stars. Our quest, our earth walk, is to look within, to know who we are, to see that we are connected to all things, that there is no separation…only in the mind.*

Epilogue:
Our Soul Virtues

It has occurred to me on many occasions that folks often puzzle as to ways of following virtues of Spirit. We tend to engage each day with good intentions but become quickly distracted as the ego's operations in the third dimension become more acute. We seem to easily fall into the routine that the ego suggests without focusing on the quality of Spirit and the intuition that is provided through our authentic Self. Consequently, we trundle through each day without the mindfulness of our Spirit Virtues—those infinite directions that point us towards our daily purpose. Instead, the distractions of the third-dimension somehow seem to exert more power than that of our Spirit messages. This process of distraction is not uncommon to us, yet intrinsically begs us to be mindful of the spiritual needs to be examined. Consider, for example, the following.

Many of us love the rhapsodic and smooth dulcet tones of the late crooner Frank Sinatra. His deep melodic voice and the projected warmth in his many songs allow us to retreat from our daily reality and bask in the rich combination of his voice, music, and spirit. One of the more memorable phrases he uttered in his songs was the trailing *do be do be do's* that often sent us into a deep space of relaxation as his voice drifted towards his musical conclusion.

I often wonder if Sinatra knew the significance of his melodic *do be do be do's*? As we listen to the wisdom of the ancient sages and mystics, we have consistently been instructed to BE, rather than DO. In other words, according to the ancients, we don't have to DO anything to achieve ascension, but rather just BE. This can be a difficult concept for us to embrace in our three-dimensional world inasmuch we are a DOING species. The true path for each of us is really about simply BEING. There are, indeed, few things, if any, we have to DO. We do need is to be able to understand the nature of what BEING spiritually consists. Actually, it is incredibly simple. BEING is just that—BEING, not DOING. One must stop thinking about what one thinks one must *do* and just bask in the gifts the universe continually supplies.

We might take a moment to enjoy the fragrance of a flower, or simply become immersed within the sounds of running water in a pristine stream. BEING can also be a walk in the woods or basking in any other peaceful setting and only focusing on the sounds of the moment. It is a case of letting go of your thinking, letting go of your thoughts, dropping your expectations of what should be and accept what *is*. Your BEING will contribute to what *is* by simply acknowledging your own deep surrender and attention to what is.

I have displayed in the next segment some concepts of BEING that one can hold within the expressions of essential *Virtues of Spirit*. I invite you to print them out and carry them along with you each day to ponder their significance. You may use them as a moment to moment prayer, a deep meditation and/or a reminder of the *Virtues of Spirit* reflected in simply BEING.

My Virtues of Spirit

I have GRATITUDE for all that is.

I offer FORGIVENESS to all, for all, including myself.

I extend COMPASSION to all God's creatures.

I exhibit PATIENCE and ignore the illusion of time.

*I choose SURRENDER to what IS and embrace
the power of Spirit.*

Thus, Spirit immerses me within the sweet perfume of

UNCONDITIONAL LOVE…and permeates my Soul.

Integral Thoughts to Enlightenment

72 *Things I've Learned ...And Counting*

By David DiPietro Weiss

1. Life proceeds according to our intention for it.

2. You only hear what you are ready to hear and only understand that which you are ready to understand.

3. We must continually remind ourselves of who we authentically are.

4. We are eternal spiritual beings in a temporary physical form.

5. What we take to be reality is the product of our thoughts and beliefs

6. We are a physical extension of Source energy.

7. We are vibrational beings in a vibrational universe.

8. Our emotions are vibrational interpreters.

9. The Law of Attraction is the most powerful Law in the universe.

10. If you desire it, the universe will produce it.

11. Without asking, you will receive no answer.

12. We are vibrational transmitters and receivers.

13. Your powerful beliefs were once gentle thoughts.

14. The longer we think thoughts, the stronger they become.

15. Emotions are indicators of your point of attraction.

16. It's not about controlling thoughts, it's about guiding thoughts.

17. Your attention to joy invites it in.

18. It is impossible to control conditions that others have created.

19. Some things you knew before you arrived. The proclivity of your gifts and talents were brought in with you, to be developed further here.

20. You are here because you have a purpose. Seek your purpose!

21. You bring with you the karma of your past lives/both positive & negative.

22. Your greatest gift to give is happiness to yourself.

23. You must be selfish enough to align with well-being.

24. Behind every desire is the desire to feel good.

25. Pay attention to your intentions.

26. Everyone, every creature you meet each day, is a HOLY encounter.

27. The only true prayer is one of gratitude…for what IS.

28. Our physical life is an illusion. There is a *Reality* that is beyond this transitory physical existence.

29. We must learn to love what IS…

30. We must learn to minimize or eliminate expectations.

31. *They* get to do that. *You* get to choose your reactions; to judge or appreciate.

32. The idea of having multiple existences (reincarnation) is not any stranger that the fact that one was born into this one in the first place.

33. If you possess happiness, you possess everything.

34. The power to be happy comes through meditation and prayer.

35. Happiness depends chiefly on your personal attitude. Happiness is a decision. Decide now to be of the state of happiness, and all else will follow.

36. We must strive to forgive, first ourselves and then all others.

37. We *live* in a three dimensional world as our Spirit *lives* within and above this dimension.

38. Love is not the physical love as we define it; it is the embracing of the concept that we are all One and loving ourselves as One.

39. There is only ONE of us here! We do not exist as separate entities *except* in the illusion of the third dimension.

40. There are many paths in the journey of enlightenment; your path is the right one for you at this time.

41. Say not that I have found THE truth; rather say that I have found A truth.

42. Say not that I have found the path of the Soul; say rather that I have found the Soul while walking on my path.

43. We reincarnate from one body to another depending upon our desires and planning while in the higher dimension spirit worlds.

44. We co-create our lives in the space between lives and make a bargain not to remember the choices for life we made while in that realm.

45. Life becomes a matter of inspired choices to address those karmic debts and rewards that we carry with us; and each incarnation is an opportunity for us to address that karma. The inspiration of choice comes from intuition.

46. Each incarnation brings us the challenges we need and face in our latest incarnate state of being.

47. If we don't make the choice that heals separation, the same situation will present itself again and again, either in the current life or in yet another life with a similar situation, until we satisfy the contract with our Soul to eradicate separation.

48. First there is intent, then desire, then will, and then manifestation.

49. There are many dimensions in our spiritual existence. We *physically* live in the third dimension…height, width and depth. Time is irrelevant in the 4th dimension yet it is the quasi-entry into our non-physical dimensions. The 5th dimension begins our true non-physical dimension and the 6th fully engages our non-physical state.

50. Death is not the opposite of life; Death is the opposite of birth. Death is the birthing back into the Spirit world.

51. Prayer is the opportunity to talk to God; Meditation is when we are in silence and allow God the opportunity to talk to us.

52. Life is a series of choices; one can *choose* to be happy, sad, healthful and joyful.

53. There is only *NOW*. There is no past, no future. In *NOW*, there is no time. It is our link to eternity.

54. How we face each chosen challenge determines our progress on the path of enlightenment and ascension.

55. Enlightenment is a process and a journey, not a destination.

56. Love, Gratitude, Abundance, Compassion, Surrender, patience, and Forgiveness are the *stuff* of our learning practices.

57. There is a *process* of ascension that naturally unfolds when one is willing to commit to the work.

58. The first thing to do each day is to be joyful and anticipate a wonderful day…and allow it to manifest.

59. Man proposes, God disposes; Sometimes God proposes and Man disposes.

60. Offer your desires, preferences, and your willingness, but do not be *attached* to the outcome.

61. All actions within the universe are calculated to the highest good. The highest good may or may not be parallel to that for which we pray.

62. Strive to be aware at all times and to still one's monkey mind that swings from thought to thought.

63. Thought is NOT the key to enlightenment.

64. In this the third dimension, there are but two emotions: Love and Fear. Love, however, is not the opposite of fear. Love simply is and can have no opposite.

65. Life is energy. We are energy beings and, according to quantum physics, we attract what we think.

66. *Everything* in the universe consists of the same stuff; molecules, atoms and space; the same energy packets that comprise us.

67. Our cells consist of molecules. Molecules are made of atoms. Atoms consist of sub-atomic electrons, protons and neutrons. We all consist of packets of energy made up of these sub-atomic particles. These packets of energy are the *stuff* of the universe. Sub-atomic particles are not made up of energy. *They are energy.*

68. The only difference between you and other physical objects and living things in our world is how these sub-atomic particles are grouped together into differing objects and how they vibrate.

69. A sub-atomic particle is not always a particle. It is not necessarily an object, such as a grain of sand, as we are taught to believe. Sub-atomic particles are, in fact, *probabilities* of existence.

70. Because sub-atomic particles are probabilities of existence, they are more *potential* than objects. They may have multiple existences—depending on how they are viewed. They can be particles or waves, be in two places at once, or exist in parallel universes.

71. By one's thoughts, one can influence or determine the probabilities. That is, when one observes the energy, one influences the outcome. By observing, one can affect the present and future. Such is the marvel of Quantum Physics. The reason that the sub-atomic particles band together in a particular object is due to our group or individual observation and thought. The outcome is the result of interaction of everyone's thoughts.

72. Quantum Mechanics (Physics) shows that we can deliberately, consciously, alone, or with groups, fashion our world with the power of thought. Wow! What a concept!

A Pre-Meditation Prayer...
I Am That I Am

I am that I am
I am not the body
I am not the emotions
I am not the thoughts
I am not the mind
The mind is only subtle
Instument of the soul
I am the soul
I am a spiritual being of
Divine Intelligence
Divine love, divine power
I am ONE with the Higher Soul
I am that I am
I am one with the divine spark
I am a child of spirit
I am connected with spirit
I am one with spirit
I am ONE with all

—Master Choa Kok Sui

www.ingramcontent.com/pod-product-compliance
Lightning Source LLC
Chambersburg PA
CBHW022123040426
42450CB00006B/827